What Do I Own and What Owns Me ?

A Spirituality of Stewardship

What Do I Own

and

What Owns Me?

A Spirituality
of Stewardship

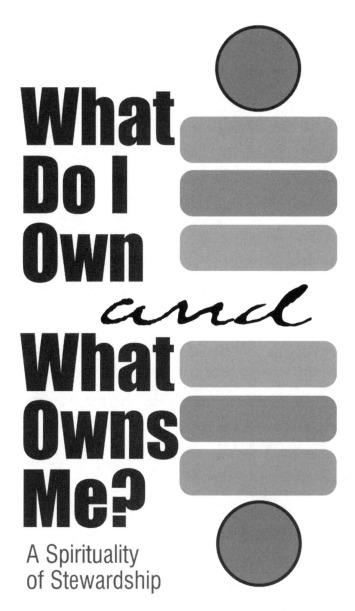

Daniel Conway

TWENTY
THIRD *23rd*
PUBLICATIONS

Inspired by and Dedicated to
Archbishop Thomas J. Murphy (1932-1997),
and with special thanks to my wife, Sharon, and family.
In Christo gaudium et spes.

Second printing 2006

Twenty-Third Publications
A Division of Bayard
1 Montauk Avenue, Suite 200
New London, CT 06320
(860) 437-3012 or (800) 321-0411
www.23rdpublications.com

ISBN-10:1-58595-393-8
ISBN: 978-1-58595-393-6

Library of Congress Catalog Card Number: 2004097964
Printed in the U.S.A.

Contents

List of Abbreviations

RPL: *Reflections on the Pastoral Letter.* A transcription of a videotaped address by Archbishop Thomas J. Murphy given in Indianapolis, Indiana, November 29, 1993. (A version of this address was published in the proceedings of the Roman Catholic Conference on Stewardship: Co-Sponsored by Lilly Endowment Inc. and the Archdiocese of Indianapolis, November 29, 1993. This publication is no longer available in print, so all references use the videotape transcript which is included in this publication as an Appendix) A DVD version of this presentation is included with this book

SDR: *Stewardship: A Disciple's Response,* United States Conference of Catholic Bishops, Washington, DC, 1992. Tenth anniversary edition, December 2002.

GH: "Giving from the Heart" in ***The Practice of Stewardship in Religious Fundraising,*** *New Directions in Philanthropic Fundraising,* Volume 17, Fall 1997. Jossey-Bass Publishers, San Francisco, California.

Introduction

My first private conversation with Archbishop Thomas J. Murphy took place in 1990 in Seattle. I was beginning a research project (the findings of which were eventually published as *The Reluctant Steward*) whose purpose was to examine the attitudes of pastors and seminary leaders on faith and money. As a former rector of the Archdiocese of Chicago's major seminary (St. Mary-of-the-Lake, Mundelein, Illinois), and the newly appointed chairman of the United States Catholic bishops' ad hoc committee on stewardship, Archbishop Murphy was at the top of my list of persons to interview.

It was not easy to schedule an appointment with him. He had an administrative assistant, but he kept his own calendar and was difficult to pin down. After multiple phone calls and many proposed and rejected dates, I finally got an appointment. I was told that the only slot available on the archbishop's calendar was a Wednesday morning breakfast meeting at a hotel in downtown Seattle (within walking distance of St. James Cathedral and the Chancery office). I was advised that the archbishop's time was limited and that I should be prompt.

I remember two things about my first personal encounter with Archbishop Murphy: his passion for stewardship and his personal warmth and gracious hospitality. I was keenly aware of his limited time, but he never gave any indication that he was in a hurry. In fact, he was so caught up in the discussion of "sturdship" (as he pronounced it) that he acted like he had all the time in the world.

During this one-hour interview, the archbishop taught me about stewardship—using anecdotes, stories, and personal examples that I would later hear over and over again in his Diocesan Stewardship Day talks and in the presentations he made during the International Catholic Stewardship Council's (ICSC) Institute for Stewardship and Development. The core of this stewardship message is summarized in this book of reflections—especially in the chapter headings, quotes, and "sidebar" stories. The majority of these are taken from a talk (captured on videotape) given in Indianapolis in November 1993 to representatives from the five Catholic dioceses of Indiana. Additional quotes are taken from his final reflections on stewardship, which were published posthumously in the fall of 1997 in a chapter entitled, "Giving from the Heart" (GH) in *The Practice of Stewardship in Religious Fundraising*, Volume 17 of *New Directions in Philanthropic Fundraising*, a professional journal sponsored by the Center on Philanthropy at Indiana University and Jossey-Bass Publishers.

Always Powerful
During the seven years I was blessed to know him, I heard Archbishop Murphy give his stewardship talk (or some variation of it) at least fifteen times—in parish halls, hotel conference rooms, retreat houses, and seminaries from Baltimore to Chicago to Orlando to Indianapolis to Los Angeles. I have now watched his videotaped talk at least thirty times—on wide-screen projection equipment in state-of-the-art auditoriums and on thirteen-inch monitors with tinny audio in cavernous old parish gymnasiums. The message is always powerful. The audience reaction is always the same. Archbishop Murphy's passion for stewardship is contagious!

As a result of this immersion into his teaching, which began during breakfast in that Seattle hotel a dozen years ago, I have come to the conclusion that his stewardship message can be summarized in one two-part question: *What do I own, and what owns me?* He posed this question to me during our breakfast interview, and he kept on asking it for the next seven years until he was taken from us (too soon by our reckoning) on June 26, 1997.

What do I own, and what owns me? In Chapter 7, I offer a more detailed reflection on the importance of this question. Here let me simply say that I believe this question is the key to the understanding and practice of stewardship as a way of life. Archbishop Murphy was keenly aware that, in the final analysis, he owned (or controlled) nothing, and was, instead, owned (or possessed) wholly and completely by "a good and gracious God." This basic insight permeates all his teaching, and I believe it is the heart of the stewardship message that he sought to convey in his talks, written reflections, and (above all) in the work of the U.S. Bishops' Committee on Stewardship.

Personal Experience

At the time that I first came to know Archbishop Murphy—and was privileged to teach with him and travel with him throughout the United States—his most powerful illustration of the stewardship message was his personal experience of major surgery in Chicago in the 1970s (Chapter 7).

As I was wheeled into the surgical room, it suddenly dawned on me: "You know, when you're in that surgical room it doesn't matter who you are. It doesn't matter one darn bit what you own. What matters at that moment in time is a competent surgical team and a good and gracious God" (RPL).

To surrender control (or the illusion of control) and trust in the generous God who has given us everything we have, and all that we are, is the sum and substance of stewardship as "a lifestyle that reflects who we are and what we believe" (Chapters 3 and 10).

At the end of his life, when he was dying from leukemia, Archbishop Murphy's witness to stewardship became much more profound. But it was the same message: life is a gift to be cherished, shared, and given back to the Lord with increase. In the end, we will be held accountable not for who we are (our status, prestige, or accomplishments) and not for what we possess (houses, cars, bank balances, or stock portfolios). Instead, we will be asked to render an account of our taking and giving (Chapter 9). Over and over Archbishop Murphy asked: Have you shared yourself (and your possessions) generously with others—because it's the right thing to do and because you really want to? Have you nurtured and developed all God's gifts and returned them with increase? Can you honestly say that you have lived a lifestyle of sharing and, so, have built a holy place within your life, your parishes, your diocese, your church (Chapter 10)?

A Pastoral Vision

In this book of reflections, I deliberately refer to Archbishop Murphy's "stewardship message." He did not formulate a theology of stewardship, but as a bishop, he articulated a pastoral vision of stewardship as a way of life, and he communicated that vision in many ways. Surely the most significant and enduring way was through his leadership role in the development and publication of the U.S. Catholic Bishops' 1992 pastoral letter, *Stewardship: A Disciple's Response* (SDR).

The archbishop believed that the stewardship pastoral

could be summarized in a sentence from St. Paul's letter to the Thessalonians: "What God wants is for all of you to be holy" (1 Thes 4:3). For him the pastoral letter was designed to be a spiritual reflection on the call to live a holy life in today's world. As such, it is a powerful expression of the bishops' stewardship message to citizens of a wealthy, powerful nation facing many questions about its identity and role in the waning years of a troubled century.

Archbishop Murphy took delight in the fact that this pastoral letter doesn't look like a church document. It's too easy to read and understand! He was also proud of the fact that the pastoral only mentions finances twice in its entire sixty-four pages (Chapter 10)! It is a pastoral (and, in many ways, poetic) expression of the vision that was at the core of Archbishop Murphy's stewardship message. It is not systematic theology, biblical study, or even catechetical instruction. Rather, it is a spiritual reflection on the way mature disciples are called to follow Jesus Christ—without counting the cost. It is a reflection on the journey to holiness that is at the heart of Christian life.

Individuals or groups who look to the pastoral letter to provide practical guidelines on church fundraising or finances are bound to be disappointed. It is not what many people expected, because stewardship as we look at it and reflect on it goes beyond the mere sharing of financial gifts. It asks us to do something that is far more difficult, and that is to share ourselves (Chapter 3).

A Rare Gift

Thomas J. Murphy was given a rare gift. He could inspire others with his passion for stewardship, as something far more radical than fundraising, as one of the chief characteristics of what it means to be a disciple of Jesus Christ, as a call to faith and conversion, and as a source of grace and deepening spirituality. The archbishop was a good steward of this precious gift, and the pastoral letter is his legacy!

When my breakfast interview with Archbishop Murphy was finished, I began to put away my things—conscious of the archbishop's limited time. "What do you have scheduled for the rest of the morning?" he asked me. I told him that I planned to return to my hotel room and write up my notes.

He said, "Come with me to the chancery. I want you to meet Archbishop Hunthausen and the great people who work in our stewardship office!"

So, off we went, walking up the hill overlooking Puget Sound, still talking about stewardship, and when we arrived at the chancery, Archbishop Murphy personally gave me a tour of the building and introduced me to everyone we met along the way! I felt like a prodigal son returned at last from a faraway land (and a lifestyle that could hardly be called good stewardship). Three hours later, I said goodbye to Archbishop Murphy and returned to my hotel room.

I Became a Disciple

Without realizing it, I became a disciple of Archbishop Murphy at that first breakfast together. He had won me over (lock, stock, and barrel) with his passion for stewardship and his amazing hospitality. There would be many more meetings—at the ICSC conferences and institutes, at seminars, in cars and on airplanes. (We even went through a Los Angeles mudslide together on our way from the airport to St. John's Seminary in Camarillo. We arrived at the seminary long after the time for our evening presentations, but Archbishop Murphy's reputation was such that all classes were cancelled the next morning and we received the students'—and the faculty's—undivided attention!) On each of these occasions, I had a similar experience of his passion and his hospitality. I also heard him ask himself, me, and everyone else in the room, What do I own and what owns me?

Archbishop Murphy taught me that stewardship means letting go of my independence, my ego, my need for control, and my desire to "be someone." He showed me that true stewardship means that I depend on a good and gracious God for who I am and what is mine—because they are all gifts to me. He illustrated his powerful stewardship message with funny stories, personal examples, and whatever media he had access to (videotapes, paintings, poetry, even Peanuts cartoons). One of his favorite quotes was from an artist in the Pacific Northwest who painted nativity scenes in contemporary settings. Regarding the artist's depiction of the birth of Jesus as an infant born to poverty and homelessness, shivering in his mother's arms, the archbishop quotes the artist, saying, "We are invited to hold a shivering God within our hands, and that shivering God, in turn, holds us" (Chapter 8).

Two Objectives

My hope is to accomplish two objectives with this book of reflections. First, I want to underscore some important stewardship themes in the pastoral letter and in the archbishop's teaching, itself. And second, I want to help carry the stewardship message beyond the point where he had to let go of it (and entrust it to our care).

Archbishop Murphy taught that stewardship invites us to assume a lifestyle of sharing, and in the divine economy, to discover the richness of finding God. May we find this abundance of grace and deepening spirituality in the Scriptures, in the pastoral letter on stewardship, and in the words and example of this good and gracious steward.

Chapter 1

A Source of Grace and Deepening Spirituality

Many of us are caught up with numerous committee meetings—and far be it from me to say that committee meetings can't be a source of grace or a source of deepening spirituality! But I do have to let you know immediately that over the last four or five years working with this [the bishops' stewardship] committee and meeting many of the people involved with stewardship has perhaps been one of the most exciting, tremendous experiences of my life. In fact, I can tell you honestly it has made a difference in my life. It has made me reflect on basic values, basic beliefs, and basic convictions, which are not only something I have to believe with my head, but something that makes a difference in my heart.

+Thomas Murphy

Grace is the constant outpouring of God's unconditional love. It is the generous reaching out to others that is an integral part of God's essential nature as the creator and sustainer of all life. Stewardship is a source of grace, because it reminds us that God never stops giving and that everything we have (and all that we are) comes to us as God's free gift.

The pastoral letter, *Stewardship: A Disciple's Response*, describes a Christian steward as "one who receives God's gifts gratefully, cherishes and tends them in a responsible and accountable manner, and returns them with increase to the Lord" (SDR, p. 9). Because God never stops giving, a Christian steward is constantly being invited (and challenged) to receive, cherish, share, and return with increase the fruits of God's abundant generosity. This is why stewardship is a lifelong responsibility. As long as God keeps giving, we are called to be open and responsive to his gifts (his grace).

Letting Go
Stewardship is a source of deepening spirituality because it challenges us to let go of any false notions that we are somehow in control of our lives, our skills and talents, or our material possessions. We are not the authors of our own existence. We are not the owners of our spiritual and material gifts. We are stewards (caretakers or custodians) of what belongs exclusively and entirely to God.

God has given us the gift of life. Our response should be to praise God for this great treasure and to demonstrate our gratitude by taking care of (and sharing) this wonderful gift. We have received the gift of intelligence. We are responsible for developing our minds and growing in wisdom and understanding.. We have been given the skills and abilities that allow us to earn a living, care for those we love, and contribute to the common good by our work and by our service to others in the Church and in our community. These gifts of time and talent make it possible for us to acquire the material possessions that we need and enjoy. All of God's gifts are good. They are meant to be used responsibly and shared generously with others.

Stewardship is a source of grace when it helps us develop a lifestyle of sharing. When we respond to God's goodness by growing in gratitude, responsibility and generosity, we can experience the difference that stewardship makes in our daily lives. As the archbishop said so often, stewardship invites us to reflect on what is most basic and fundamental in our lives—and to respond from the heart. Stewardship is not a program. It is a way of life. It requires nourishment and practice. A Christian steward is one who makes a conscious decision to remain open to God's grace and to respond generously (from the heart) to whatever opportunities and challenges may come.

Recognizing God
In his final reflections on stewardship, Archbishop Murphy acknowledged that even leukemia can be seen as a gift from God. He recognized the workings of a good and gracious God in the dedication and skill of the healthcare professionals who treated him and in the outpouring of love and support he received from family, friends and people throughout the Church of Western Washington (especially the school children who donated blood in his name). He even saw God's hand in the anxiety and fear that forced him to reaffirm his basic values, basic beliefs, and basic convictions.

Last year, just after Thanksgiving, I was diagnosed with acute myelogenous leukemia and related kidney disorders. I underwent a long hospitalization, and during this period it did not matter who I was or what I owned. All that mattered then was the skill of my healthcare professionals and the providence of a good and gracious God! Now that I am out of the hospital and feeling well (in spite of going to the doctor and the hospital for transfusions of blood and platelets on a regular basis) I have a whole new awareness of what stewardship means (GH, p. 28).

Stewardship helps us recognize that both the ordinary experiences of daily living and the most profound moments of our life and death are gifts from God to be cherished and shared with others. Since God never stops giving, our opportunities to respond from the heart are truly endless. That's why stewardship is a way of life—and a lifelong source of grace and deepening spirituality.

Questions for Reflection and Discussion

1. What is your understanding of grace? How do you experience God's grace working in your life?

2. Have you experienced stewardship as a source of grace and deepening spirituality? In what ways? How has this changed you? What does he mean by this? What examples does he use to illustrate this conviction?

3. Do you think there is a connection between stewardship and spirituality? How does this affect you on a daily basis? What difference does it make in your daily life?

4. "Stewardship is not a program. It is a way of life." What do you think this statement means?

Chapter 2

Far More Radical than Fundraising

The biggest question that the Committee on Stewardship tried to face was, "How do we respond to these needs; how do we respond to the gospel message of Jesus Christ in a sustained, workable way?" The Committee on Stewardship knew it could raise the consciousness of people to these dramatic needs and encourage them to respond. The committee also knew that there are many ways in which the professional fundraisers could help the Church ask people for greater support. In fact, Bishop McManus said at one of our early meetings, "We could finish our task right away by calling the committee, instead of one on stewardship, of calling it a committee on fundraising." We could publish all the wonderful work that has been done by the professional people and share it with the dioceses and parishes in our country. Yet, the Committee on Stewardship envisioned its task as something far more radical, far more fundamental.

+ Thomas Murphy

There is an inherent danger in describing stewardship as a source of grace and spirituality. We may find ourselves so wrapped up in the spirituality of stewardship that we neglect its practical implications. After all, stewardship is a practical virtue like hospitality. You can't just think good stewardship. You have to put it into action!

The impetus for the U.S. bishops' pastoral letter on stewardship was the financial crisis facing the Catholic Church in the United States in the late 1980s (two decades after the close of the Second Vatican Council). Dramatic changes in the Church and in society had placed new demands on parishes, schools, and other Catholic institutions, and for reasons that are still not completely clear, funding for the Church's work failed to keep pace with the increasing costs. In response to this crisis, Archbishop Murphy raised the issue at an administrative board meeting of the United States Conference of Catholic Bishops (USCCB). The result of this intervention was an ad hoc committee, chaired by him, charged with studying the issue and proposing solutions.

A Spiritual Crisis

Archbishop Murphy never lost sight of the fact that resources (human and financial) are essential to the Church's ministry and that they do not ordinarily fall from heaven like the manna that fed the Jewish people in the desert. At the same time, he was absolutely convinced that the root cause of the church's failure to generate new or increased resources was a spiritual crisis (a crisis of faith and conversion), not a financial crisis. He illustrated this conviction by calling attention to people's amazing generosity in response to emergency situations or natural disasters. "What is amazing, my friends, is that we respond to the emergency situation, and we feel good about it. But long after the emergency ends, the hunger is still there; the homelessness is still there; the flooding is still there."

This insight into the sporadic nature of Catholics' generosity led the bishops on the ad hoc committee to formulate their task in a way that was different from what some people expected. The bishops on the ad hoc committee might have chosen to ask an eminently practical question, such as: How can we raise more money to meet the growing needs of our dioceses, parishes, schools, social service agencies, and missionary work?

The committee might have accomplished its task relatively quickly and successfully by posing this question and then calling attention to the proven principles and techniques of professional fundraising. Instead, they posed for themselves a different kind of question. They asked: How do we respond to the Gospel message of Jesus Christ in a sustained, workable way? It was still a practical question (they were looking for a "workable way"), but the committee sought a solution that was deeper and more long-lasting than an immediate response to the church's urgent financial needs.

A Graced Moment
The committee's decision to ask this more fundamental question was a graced moment in the life of the church. It meant that the committee would reject the quick fix and pursue a task far more radical, far more fundamental. Its decision to take what some called the high road of spirituality (rather than the low road of finance or fundraising) was not appreciated by everyone—including some members of the hierarchy and some lay leaders who helped underwrite the committee's work. Even after the pastoral letter was approved by the body of bishops and distributed to parishes and dioceses throughout the United States,

some questioned the letter's exclusive focus on the spiritual and pastoral dimensions of stewardship rather than the church's continuing financial problems. They suggested that it was necessary to deal with immediate financial problems first and then to address the spirituality aspect. The committee argued that if you start with money (or put too much emphasis on the church's need for resources), all you get is a short-lived financial response—like an increased offertory program in a parish that produces a temporary spike in giving but no fundamental change in the way parishioners live their daily lives or participate personally in the mission and ministry of the church.

I agree with the bishops' decision to focus their pastoral letter on the spirituality of stewardship. Bishops are pastors, not professional fundraisers; their focus should be on the broader and deeper pastoral issues that concern the Christian community. But I also believe that the spiritual principles that are so beautifully expressed in *Stewardship: A Disciple's Response* can only achieve their radical, fundamental objectives if they are put into practice "in a sustained, workable way" that includes addressing the Church's very real need for increased human and financial resources.

One thing is certain. Archbishop Murphy would never have supported a plan that placed fundraising before stewardship. He would have enthusiastically supported efforts to develop new human and financial resources, but he would have insisted that priority be given to something far more radical, far more fundamental: the opportunities and challenges of teaching stewardship as a way of life!

Questions for Reflection and Discussion

1. Do you agree that stewardship is about "something far more radical, far more fundamental" than finances or fundraising? Why? Why not?

2. Do you think the Catholic Church is facing a spiritual crisis? A financial crisis? If so, how might you respond?

3. "There is no quick fix for the Church's urgent resource needs (human and financial)." How do you respond to this statement?

4. What practical suggestions can you offer for putting principles of Christian stewardship into practice in "a sustained, workable way"?

Chapter 3

A Lifestyle That Reflects What We Believe

Stewardship is part of faith. It is one of the chief characteristics of what it means to be a disciple of Jesus.
Stewardship is a lifestyle that reflects who we are and
what we believe. My friends, in many ways...that whole
question of who we are and what we believe is what this
pastoral letter is about. It is about asking us to look at our
hearts and our minds and to experience the conversion to
which we are called....Because stewardship, as we look
at it and we reflect upon it, goes beyond sharing one's
resources; it goes beyond the mere sharing of financial
gifts that have been given to us. It asks us to do something
far more difficult, and that is to share ourselves. To share
our time, our abilities, our ministry, our relationships.
Stewardship is really a call to be a holy people.

+Thomas Murphy

Stewardship is not a program. It's a way of life. What does this mean—practically speaking? Most dioceses in the United States now have some kind of stewardship education program. Many parishes have formed stewardship committees that coordinate year-round stewardship activities and annual stewardship renewals. Companies like Our Sunday Visitor and RSI Catholic Services Group have made substantial investments in stewardship education materials and stewardship enhancement initiatives. The International Catholic Stewardship Council sponsors an annual stewardship conference, regional stewardship days, and the weeklong Institute for Stewardship and Development that is held twice a year—in January and July.

A Way of Life

If stewardship is not a program, why do we need all these activities, materials, conferences, committee meetings, and enhancement initiatives? Isn't there a contradiction here between the pastoral letter's emphasis on stewardship as a form of spirituality and what might be called the bureaucratization of stewardship? Is stewardship really a way of life, or is it just another program—the church's latest fad?

I remember listening to the archbishop speak at one of the early ICSC Institutes held at the San Damiano Retreat in Danville, California. He was telling his story about "calving" in eastern Montana (see sidebar, p.23), and, as always, he brought down the house. (The calving story still provokes heartfelt laughter every time his videotaped presentation is shown—no matter who is in the audience or what the circumstances are. It is a genuinely funny story told with the archbishop's characteristic wit and self-deprecating humor.) But as I listened to this story for perhaps the third time, I couldn't help asking myself, "What does this have to do with stewardship? It's a wonderful story, and I love it, but how does it illustrate the pastoral letter and its message?"

The calving story comes at a point in the talk when Archbishop Murphy has stressed the importance of faith and conversion and the need to speak to people in their own language and on their own terms. The calving story shows the cultural differences between the Chicago-born bishop and the sixteen-year-old farm boy from Harlem, Montana. But, more importantly, it makes clear that it is the bishop himself (the "expert" on stewardship) who still has a few things to learn about the gift of life and about the power of God's grace at work in our everyday lives.

Too much stewardship talk is focused on formulas like "time, talent, and treasure" or "proportionate giving," when it should be expressed in the language and imagery of everyday life. To borrow a phrase from Tip O'Neill, a charismatic Irish American himself, all stewardship is local.

Daily Living

Stewardship is a lifestyle that reflects who we are and what we believe, and this involves daily living—not diocesan or parish programs. A commitment to stewardship should influence our most basic choices: how we spend our free time; how we develop and use the skills and abilities God has given us; and how we earn, save, spend, and share our money. This is "time, talent, and treasure" to be sure, but it is expressed in terms of daily living, not just as a formula for volunteerism or church support.

Stewardship should guide our choices: about what we do on the weekend; about the books we read and the movies we see; about how we celebrate Christmas; about how we dispose of our trash; about how we share ourselves and our material possessions with others; about how much we drink;

about relationships and sex; and, yes, about how much we contribute to the Sunday collection and the Annual Bishop's Appeal. A commitment to stewardship as a way of life should have an impact on everything we choose to do—no exceptions. This is not just another gimmick to raise funds or encourage volunteerism. It is a radical re-thinking of our everyday lives based on fundamental principles of faith and spirituality.

Stewardship challenges us to look at our hearts and minds and to experience the conversion to which we are called. This conversion is not a superficial change in our giving habits (although proportionate, sacrificial giving can be a powerful sign of a more radical change in attitude or lifestyle). A genuine conversion to stewardship means seeing everything differently (with new eyes) and acknowledging that everything we have comes to us from God as a gift to be cared for responsibly and shared generously with others.

At the International Catholic Stewardship Conference held in Rome in 2003, clergy and lay representatives from different continents and diverse cultures gathered to pray and reflect on basic principles of Christian stewardship. This conference—as wonderful as it was—was not stewardship. Stewardship is what we do when we go home to Nigeria, England, or the Americas. It is how we live each day. It is the choices we make and the lifestyles we live—not just on Sunday but every day, one day at a time, one choice at a time, until a good and gracious God calls us home and asks for an accounting of who we are, what we believe, and how we have lived. This is summed up in St. Paul's letter to the Thessalonians: "We urge you and appeal to you in the Lord Jesus to make more and more progress in the kind of life you are meant to live, the life God wants. What God wants is for all of you to be holy" (1 Thes 4:1–3).

The call to holiness is at the heart of stewardship. This is the guiding principle. Are our stewardship activities faithful to the fundamental call to be a holy people? In any of your stewardship approaches, in your parishes, for yourself, for your diocese, for the church in our country; if any approach we take does not ask us or challenge us to be a holy people, then we are not faithful to stewardship.

Questions for Reflection and Discussion

1. "Stewardship is a lifestyle that reflects who we are and what we believe." Do you agree or disagree?

2. How can we make sure that stewardship programs and activities don't get in the way of stewardship as a way of life?

3. How do we avoid overusing stewardship formulas like "time, talent, and treasure" and instead talk about stewardship in the language and images of everyday life?

4. How can a commitment to stewardship guide our choices on a day-to-day basis? How does this help us to become a holy people?

Calving in Eastern Montana

Let me tell you a story from my days as a bishop in eastern Montana. I was in a town called Harlem. It was not a major metropolitan center; in fact, it wasn't much of anything. In fact, the rectory was so small you couldn't stay there overnight with the pastor. So he had arranged for me to stay with this farm family about six miles outside of town.

The family was very nice and very good. I was given a room in a separate trailer outside the main house where two of the older boys also had their rooms and, so, there was a bath and a room and everything there was very nice and the boys took care of me. We had pizza and pop and stuff and went to bed about ten o'clock.

Anyway, right before I went to bed, Brian, the oldest, knocked on the door and said, "You know, Bishop, tonight we are probably going to have calves. So if you would like, come out to the barn to see us having calves."

And so I politely said, "Why don't you knock gently on the door and let me know if it's happening."

So Brian said, "Fine."

About two in the morning—to ask a 16-year-old kid to knock gently on the door is to give you some idea of the great quake in the San Andreas fault! Anyway, Brian pounded on the door, got me up, and I went out to the barn. It was February, and I will never forget it. But anyway, I went out to the barn and there was this calving going on. Again I remember this so vividly; I was watching this calving taking place and I guess I was turning white, because I had never seen it before. I still remember Brian turning to me and saying, "Bishop, ain't you ever seen calving before?"

And I all I remember saying to Brian was, "They don't do this in downtown Chicago!"

Faith and conversion—it's amazing the wisdom I shared with eastern Montana after the experience of calving! I spoke of life and resurrection in ways I never spoke of it before. Stewardship likewise requires a new vision. The stewardship vision is the ability to see with eyes of faith the need to share our resources, time, talents, and possessions in ways that enable us to recognize Christ in who we are and the gifts of time, talent, and resources we possess.

+Thomas J. Murphy

Chapter 4

Mature Discipleship

Each and every baptized person is called to be a disciple of Jesus Christ. It is not an option! It is not for a select few. Each and every person is called to be a disciple of Jesus Christ. Above and beyond this basic call to ministry and to Christian vocation, mature disciples make a conscious, firm decision carried out in action to be followers of Jesus Christ, no matter the cost to themselves. My friends, at the heart of this first principle is the universal call to holiness. And the call to holiness involves challenge, and difficulties at times. It is not easy to be a disciple of Jesus today. It is not easy to be faithful to the Gospel. It is not easy to live out in your life, or mine, what it means to walk with the Lord Jesus.

+Thomas Murphy

Stewardship: A Disciple's Response offers three basic principles or convictions that describe Christian stewardship as a way of life. The first conviction is that stewardship is intimately connected to mature Christian discipleship. Stewardship is not incidental to Christianity. It is essentially linked to the decision to follow Jesus Christ as his disciple.

This is the vocation of every baptized person: to follow Jesus Christ without counting the cost and to discover the joy that comes when we have given ourselves completely to the love of God and the service of our sisters and brothers in Christ. Each and every person is called to be a disciple of Jesus Christ. It is not an option! It is not for a select few.

A Conscious Decision

The pastoral letter on stewardship says that mature disciples make a conscious, firm decision—carried out in action—to be followers of Jesus Christ no matter what the cost to themselves. Stewardship is not what we do in the first fervor of conversion to Christ (St. Francis giving away all his material possessions—and his father's things as well!). Stewardship is what happens later—in the mature years of Christian life. It is the latter-day Franciscans struggling to live their vow of poverty with buildings to maintain and elderly friars to care for. It is ordinary families with mortgages, car payments, and school tuition seeking the right balance between a contemporary, secular lifestyle and a way of life that is characterized by simplicity and generous sharing.

Stewardship responds to these fundamental questions: What does it mean to be a disciple of Jesus Christ in an affluent, consumer-oriented society? How are we supposed to live an authentic Christian life in a culture that encourages attitudes and behaviors that are incompatible with the Gospel of Jesus Christ? It is not easy to be a disciple of Jesus today. It is not easy to be faithful to the Gospel...to live out what it means to walk with the Lord Jesus.

Stewardship helps us live out in practice the firm, conscious decision we have made to follow Christ. It guides our choices and frees us from the tyranny of "isms" (materialism, consumerism, secularism). Stewardship shows us how to live and work; how to buy and sell; how to spend and save; how to accumulate and share all the materials things that are necessary and enjoyable in life—without becoming obsessed or burdened by them. Stewardship frees us to live good, responsible lives. It helps us to be faithful to the Gospel in our daily living and to be generous in sharing all our gifts out of gratitude to God for his goodness to us.

How Disciples Live

How does a mature disciple of Christ live? The pastoral letter on stewardship gives us a descriptive answer: A Christian steward is one who receives God's gifts gratefully, cherishes and tends them in a responsible and accountable manner, shares them generously with others out of justice and love, and returns them to the Lord with increase. A mature disciple of Jesus Christ lives gratefully—offering thanks to God in many simple but genuine ways.

A mature disciple is also a responsible person who reflects in daily living a profound awareness that we are stewards (not owners) of all God's gifts and must, therefore, take special care of them. A mature disciple is generous—not in a condescending way but out of a firm conviction that God's gifts are to be shared freely with all our brothers and sisters in the family of God. Finally, as the parables of Jesus illustrate so poignantly, a mature disciple of Christ takes the gifts and talents God has given and makes them grow so that what is returned to the Lord on the last day is greater than what was received at the beginning.

The pastoral letter's first conviction is that there is a universal call to holiness—a call that at times involves difficulties and challenges. At its heart, stewardship is counter-cultural. It is a way of life that frequently contradicts values that are communicated day-in and day-out in advertising and the entertainment media.

Live Simply and Share

Where the culture urges us to accumulate and spend, stewardship calls us to live simply and share what we have with others. Where the culture encourages us to be aggressively competitive in our work (and even at play), stewardship invites us to strike a balance between competition and collaboration—and between "winning at any cost" and "letting go" in order to make time for family and community life. Where the culture celebrates doing things "my way," stewardship challenges us to discover the Lord's way and to make it our own.

What God wants is for all of you to be holy. Holiness is not some kind of excessive piety. It is wholeness, balance, gratitude, and generous sharing—all rooted in the basic commitment to follow Jesus Christ and to live as he lived, no matter where he leads us and no matter what it costs. The call to stewardship is a call to be a holy people. It is a call to take the risk of walking with Jesus.

Questions for Reflection and Discussion

1. Do you consider yourself to be a "mature disciple" of Jesus Christ? Why or why not?

2. What are some of the particular challenges involved in following Jesus in our contemporary culture?

3. How can stewardship help us to make better choices and find balance in our lives?

4. What are some of the risks associated with following Jesus today? How can stewardship help us "walk with Jesus" no matter what it costs?

Chapter 5

No Quick Fix

Beginning in conversion, a change of heart, this commitment is expressed not in a single action, nor even in a series of actions over a period of time, but in an entire way of life. It means committing one's very self to the Lord. Today, you know, we are so much into the quick-fix approach to things, but the committee decided early on not to just list all the [fund-raising] programs available. That would have been the quick fix. We would have been praised. We would have gotten good commendations. We would have resolved the issue for a moment. But our conviction was that we are not in this for the quick-fix— and that goes so much against the cultural grain.

+Thomas Murphy

The pastoral letter's second conviction is that a commitment to stewardship must be realized over time in "an entire way of life." One does not become a good steward through a single action (like writing a big check) or even a series of actions (many hours of community service). Rather, the seeds of stewardship, which are sown at baptism, must be nurtured and grown over an entire lifetime. Above all, stewardship must be practiced—in little things as well as big things—so that the four characteristics of Christian stewardship (gratitude, responsibility, generosity, and the willingness to give back with increase) become second nature. Stewardship is a lifestyle that reflects who we are and what we believe.

Clearly there was tension caused by the ad hoc committee's decision to take "the high road" (which was also the long road) and emphasize the spirituality of stewardship over the church's immediate financial needs. True, a gradual, long-term approach to stewardship might frustrate Americans who are used to more immediate solutions. But we are not in for the quick fix, and that goes so much against our grain.

Changing How We Live

The stewardship pastoral's second conviction is essential to a clear understanding of stewardship. Christian stewardship is not about solving a problem (the lack of participation in or financial support for Church ministries). It is about changing the way we live in the world of everyday life. This is why the pastoral letter links stewardship to discipleship. *Stewardship: A Disciple's Response* is first and foremost a reflection on how followers of Jesus Christ should live in the modern world. This is not a problem to be fixed; it is a way of being transformed according to the Gospel.

Christian stewardship is the lifestyle that best reflects who we are (followers of Jesus Christ) and what we believe (the Gospel) in the everyday circumstances of this particular era in the history of Christianity. Embracing this way of living— and putting it into practice—takes time. It also necessarily involves failure, repentance, and the courage to keep on trying. After all, who among us can be consistently grateful, responsible, or generous all the time? How often do we find ourselves guilty of resentment, self-pity, or the desire for more and more of what the world seems to offer (status, security, control of our own destiny)? We want to be good stewards—now. We resist the idea that this is something we must pursue, but never fully acquire, over an entire lifetime.

It goes against our grain to live out a commitment to stewardship one choice at a time: What shall I do this afternoon? Wouldn't it be great to have a home theater system in our family room? Do I really want to spend another weekend coaching youth basketball—or visiting my in-laws? There are no right or wrong answers here, just thousands of choices made every day that define who we are and what we value. How can we make these choices more effectively—in ways that are faithful to our commitment to walk with Jesus?

The pastoral letter's four characteristics can provide us with useful criteria for self-examination:

- Do my choices express my heartfelt gratitude, or do I make them grudgingly out of a sense of obligation or entitlement?

- Am I ready and willing to render an account of my decisions (how I have used all God's gifts), or do I have some things to hide (talents that have been buried or neglected or abused)?

- Am I truly generous with my time, my abilities, and my money, or do I share reluctantly and without joy?

It's a lot easier to increase my Sunday offering than it is to change my attitude about giving. It's a lot easier to sign up to be a lector or an usher than it is to honestly reexamine how I spend my free time. It's a lot easier for a pastor to schedule an increased offertory program than to talk with his parishioners about how they live and how they spend their money on a daily basis.

Stewardship is not easy. It is not a quick fix! This is the long, hard road the bishops chose when they decided to make a long-term commitment to teaching stewardship as a way of life.

Questions for Reflection and Discussion

If you had to fill out your own "stewardship report card," how would you grade yourself?

> (A) Excellent
>
> (B) Good
>
> (C) Fair
>
> (D) Poor
>
> (F) Failed

Please check all that apply

____ 1. I am a grateful person, appreciative and thankful for all God's gifts.

____ 2. I take full responsibility for all the gifts I have received from God. I care about others and about the world I live in.

____ 3. I freely share my time, my skills and talents, and my material possessions with others, because everything I am and all that I have are gifts from God that are meant to be shared.

____ 4. During my life, I have taken God's gifts and developed them so that when I die I can honestly say I have given back God's gifts with increase.

Are you satisfied with this report card? If yes, how do you plan to maintain this good record? If not, what can you do to improve your stewardship score?

The Trough Experience

In Indiana, as in every other place in the United States, there are thousands of fast-food restaurants, which give you the opportunity to appreciate the great American gift called the "trough" experience. It reminds me of the seminary days. But anyway, it is amazing how in our own culture that is one of the great gifts we have been given. The whole idea of the fast-food restaurant is merely to fulfill a biological need. How different the "trough" experience is from the experience of having dinner with your family. How different the experience is, and how rare the experience is today, for people to have a dinner experience that involves more than fulfilling a biological need, but involves conversation, enjoyment, presence, the gifts of people exchanging with each other. That is why this entire way of life is the second conviction. It is not a quick fix; it is not something I do all at once, nor can it be measured.

+Thomas J. Murphy

Chapter 6

The Power to Change
How We Live

Stewardship is an expression of discipleship with the power to change how we understand and live out our lives. Disciples who practice stewardship recognize [that] God is the origin of life, the giver of freedom, the source of all they have and are and will be. My friends, when you talk about stewardship you come to a third conviction. It is an expression of discipleship, which really asks us to put on new lenses—new lenses where we look at who we are and what we do from an entirely different perspective. And that is what stewardship is about. These basic principles are not new to any one of us. How do we appropriate them into our lives?

+Thomas Murphy

The third conviction of the U.S. bishops' pastoral letter is that a commitment to stewardship has the power to change the way we live. A mature disciple of Jesus Christ who makes a genuine commitment to walk with the Lord finds that he or she can never be the same again. Everything changes because we now see everything through new lenses—a new pair of eyes that show us the world (and ourselves) much more clearly.

For most of us, this entirely new perspective comes gradually through the daily practice of a lifelong commitment to stewardship. Slowly but surely we begin to recognize—in more than just a superficial way—that God truly is the source and goal of our lives and that we are called to nurture all God's gifts, share them with others, and return them to the Lord with increase.

This third conviction is illustrated by this conversation between Archbishop Murphy and his older brother, and by the comments that follow it.

I remember my brother called me up about a week after I turned 60, and he said, "You know, Tom, did you ever stop and think about it, now that you're 60, that if you live the average number of years of a person your age, you'll live to be 75, 76?" And [then] he said, "Did you ever realize that being 60 means that for every four years you have lived, you only have one left?" This is called Irish optimism. But it also makes me aware that, for instance, any of you who are 50, for every two years you have lived, you have one left. It's amazing, however, the perspective that gives. It is amazing how that simple remark by my brother—which I really took quite seriously and caringly because that is the way in which he shared it—that he was really trying to say to me, "You've got a gift. You've got the gift of life." And if I am able to have the fullness of that gift for 15 or 16 more years, what do I do with it? How do I use it? How do I share it? How do I take this resource, this incredible resource of life, and what do I do with it? How do I share it (RPL)?

This is a powerful illustration of the pastoral letter's third conviction that stewardship has the power to change how we understand and live our lives. It is a basic tenet of Christian spirituality that the contemplation of death helps us maintain a proper perspective on what life really means. If we reflect seriously and caringly on the few years we have left to live, to spend with family and friends, and to work and enjoy life's blessings, how different everything seems. Our daily complaints and frustrations seem petty. Our selfish thoughts and desires seem especially inappropriate. And our choices about how to use our time, how to develop our talents, and how to spend our money take on an entirely different meaning. The new lenses that we put on at baptism, and that mature through our commitment to walk with Jesus on a daily basis, gain even greater clarity and focus in our final years of life.

> When I first began to teach stewardship as a way of life, I had no idea how important this concept would become for me personally. Now, more than ever before, I can honestly say that I am extremely happy to be alive, to be able to speak, breathe, laugh, cry, and share hopes and dreams with my brothers and sisters in the church and in the human family. Over the past several months, I have been challenged to appreciate the most fundamental and valuable gift that a good and gracious God has given to me and to all of us—the gift of life (GH, p. 30).

Stewardship is first and foremost an appreciation of the gift of life that is so powerful it compels us to share this gift (and all that goes with it) with others. It has the power to change us—from the self-centered and anxiety-ridden people we are prone to become in our contemporary culture—to a free people who are grateful to be alive, filled with wonder at the goodness of God, and eager to share ourselves completely with family, friends, neighbors, and other pilgrims on the road to everlasting life.

Questions for Reflection and Discussion

1. How does a commitment to stewardship help you see the world differently—through new lenses? Can you give some examples?

2. Life is God's greatest gift. How can you show your gratitude for this gift? How can you share it with others?

3. Do you agree that stewardship has the power to change the way you live? What does this mean practically?

4. Can you summarize in your own words the stewardship pastoral's three convictions (mature discipleship, no quick fix, and the power to change how we live)?

Chapter 7

What Do I Own and What Owns Me?

As I was wheeled into the surgical room, it suddenly dawned on me, "You know, when you're in that surgical room, it doesn't matter who you are. It doesn't matter one darn bit what you own. What matters at that moment in time is a competent surgical staff and a good and gracious God." Those moments, uncertain and fragile as they are, become moments of grace. But after that particular moment, that experience of my life from which I came out very, very fortunate, it prompted me to ask another question. It prompted me to ask the question, "What do I own and what owns me?" At the heart of stewardship in my own reflections and my own search for how it touches my life it has prompted me to ask that question more than once, "What do I own and what owns me."

+Thomas Murphy

The question, *What do I own?* calls attention to all the spiritual and material gifts that we have received from a good and gracious God. The second question, *What owns me?* probes the state of our souls. Have we freely given over our life and our will to the Lord? Or are we still holding back—possessed in some way by the seductive influences of status, wealth, or the illusion of control?

The call to discipleship demands a radical response. As portrayed in the Gospel accounts, the Lord's invitation to discipleship is all-encompassing: "Go, sell what you have; give it to the poor; and come, follow me." The disciples do not fully understand the radical steps they are taking, but they are drawn by the powerful desire to walk with Jesus. They possess an intuitive understanding that his way, which will certainly require sacrifice and a whole new way of thinking, leads ultimately to freedom and an abundance of life. Although they are weak, sinful people who do not always live up to the demands placed on them, there is no question that Jesus' disciples have made a commitment to a manner of living that is, for them, radically new.

The question, *What do I own and what owns me?* provides a framework for assessing our progress in the discipleship journey. It allows us to examine our consciences and to conduct an inventory of all the gifts we have received from a good and gracious God. But most of all, the question challenges us to be honest about our commitment to stewardship as a way of life. Is this something we really believe in, or are we just along for the ride?

Stewardship challenges us to take stock of ourselves—in concrete, practical ways and in more profound ways as well. Taking stock of ourselves spiritually and materially is at the heart of stewardship:

Sure, you and I own a lot of things legally, juridically, but the question, I think, that is behind stewardship is: Of all the things that we juridically own, what owns us? What owns me? That is not only the physical things; it can be other realities; it can be relationships; it can be sexuality; it can be our dependence on liquor or drugs. It can be a thousand and one things. The critical question in stewardship is: What do I own and what owns me (RPL).

This question is not just for peak moments in our lives. On the contrary, it needs to be integrated into all aspects of daily living to help us gauge whether or not we are truly living as Christian stewards. The goal of stewardship, as a way of life, is to get to the point where we no longer have to ask what it means to be a good steward. This is the mature form of Christian discipleship described in the pastoral letter—in which gratitude, responsibility, generosity, and the willingness to give back with increase have become second nature to us. Of course, we will never get to the point where stewardship happens automatically. Stewardship is always about making choices and taking risks. But by regularly taking stock of ourselves and asking ourselves the stewardship question, we can make significant progress in our efforts to develop an attitude toward life that genuinely reflects the pastoral letter's four characteristics of Christian stewardship. Stewardship becomes a way of life when we do not have to ask the meaning of the question, "What do I own and what owns me?" but when it becomes part of our lives (RPL).

Questions for Reflection and Discussion

1. "What do I own?" List the three most significant spiritual gifts God has given you. Do the same for your most prized material possessions. Why are these important to you? How can you more effectively share these gifts with others?

2. "What owns me?" Have you completely surrendered your life and your will to God, or are you holding back? Make a list of the things that most often stand in the way of your following Jesus without counting the cost.

The Critical Question

The critical question in stewardship is: "What do I own and what owns me?"

My friends, that is a question that we have to raise for ourselves, as well as for others. This is a question that must be part of our lives. We just can't keep asking, "What does stewardship mean?"

This reminds me of a story of an anthropologist who was studying the aboriginal people in Australia. In the community in which she lived, there was a rich tradition of storytelling. The people would gather in the evening, and a story would be told and then another and another. The anthropologist felt extraordinarily privileged when she was invited to join that group.

The first story told that evening was about the ancient mythical animal ancestor of that group and its adventures in the primeval world. It was rich with detail, action, and imagery. At the end of the story, the anthropologist was delighted. "Can I ask you a question?" she said. "What does it mean?"

There was silence. All eyes were on her. The elder looked at her gravely and said, "That is the one question you cannot ask."

It was a long time before she was invited again. She had asked the wrong question. Stewardship becomes a way of life when we do not have to ask the meaning of the question, "What do I own and what owns me?" but when it becomes part of our lives.

+Thomas J. Murphy

Chapter 8

Poverty as a Spiritual Discipline

The poverty that exists in our world, the concrete poverty that affects children and young people and adults, the poverty that so often we are not aware of, and yet we are called, as disciples of Jesus, to be people committed to poverty. When I think of poverty, I think, the hardest poverty to which I am called, and I think perhaps you are too as well, is to admit at times I don't have control. The hardest poverty is not owning things; the hardest poverty is not being hungry or homeless; the hardest poverty is not being in control. For any of us not to be in control, that is poverty. Poverty means I depend on a good and gracious God for who I am and what is mine because they are gifts to me. That is the power of the feast we celebrate in a few weeks [Christmas] where, as one poet put it, we are invited to hold a shivering God within our hands, and that shivering God in turn holds us. To be open to that lack of control, to admit that I believe and I hope in a good and gracious God is truly something that stewardship makes us aware of.

+Thomas Murphy

A commitment to stewardship as a way of life necessarily involves a commitment to poverty as a spiritual discipline. Poverty means not being in control. This is certainly true for people who are materially poor and who, therefore, have little or no control over life's basic necessities (food, clothing, shelter, health care). But not being in control is something that every human being has to come to terms with eventually. The rich and the comfortable possess many things that can offer an illusion of control, but in fact, we are all entirely in God's hands—utterly dependent on the divine mercy and goodness for everything that we have and all that we are.

Depending on God

Poverty means we depend on a good and gracious God for who we are and what is ours because they are gifts to us. It is not easy to maintain a commitment to stewardship when we are constantly being asked to let go of all the things we have been taught will fulfill our most basic needs and our most natural desires—not to mention the security, success, and satisfaction promised to us by material wealth and prosperity. Stewardship asks us to forsake the control of ownership and embrace the poverty of Christian discipleship. It challenges us to really mean it when we say that God is the true owner and giver of all things; we are God's stewards.

There was an artist of the Pacific Northwest who painted a series of nativity scenes that place the Holy Family in contemporary settings of poverty and homelessness. The artist asks us to confront the stark reality of the Lord's birth without the aura of comfort and security that often surrounds it. We are challenged to see with new eyes the poverty that Jesus freely accepted for our sake (the omnipotent Son of God comes to us as a helpless, shivering infant entirely dependent on his poor, homeless parents). This is the true meaning of Christmas. We are invited to hold a shivering God within our hands, and that shivering God in turn holds us.

The spiritual discipline of poverty challenges us to acknowledge our absolute dependence on God, and then to let this radical awareness shape the way we live on a daily basis. The temptation we face is to make a commitment to stewardship in the abstract while we continue to search for control over our daily lives through an attachment to material things, social status, economic security, or the psychological comforts of a life without commitment or risk. Stewardship challenges us to ask ourselves some hard questions: What does God want me to do with all the gifts I have been given? How can I be more generous in sharing myself and my possessions with others? What can I give up for the sake of simplicity and charity?

To be open to this kind of lack of control, and to place ourselves entirely in God's hands, requires faith and conversion. This is a far more radical challenge than the sharing of resources with the church.

> There is no doubt that it is important to ask people to live a life of stewardship which is prayerful, planned, proportionate, and sacrificial. Those are the big words we use so often—prayerful, planned, proportionate, and sacrificial—when it comes to sharing one's resources with one's parish, diocese, and the universal Church. But my friends, no program, no choice of words, no stewardship appeal slogan, no brochure, no letter from the pastor—or even from the bishop—will have any long-term effect on the lives of people to encourage them to live a life of stewardship if the far more fundamental issues of faith and conversion are not addressed (RPL).

The spiritual discipline of poverty helps us put into practice a fundamental principle of our faith: that we are entirely dependent on God for everything. It also challenges us to let the grace of God transform us from our old ways of thinking and acting (the illusion of control) to a new way of living that is filled with confidence and hope.

Questions for Reflection and Discussion

1. Poverty is "not being in control." How does this definition apply to people who are materially poor (without money or material possessions)? How does it apply to those who are "poor in spirit" (those who have placed themselves entirely in God's hands)? How does it apply to you?

2. How can we assess (or measure) our commitment to stewardship? Are we stewards in name only, or do we truly acknowledge God as the owner and giver of all things? What are some concrete, practical signs that we have given up the search for control?

3. "There is no doubt that it is important to ask people to live a life of stewardship that is prayerful, planned, proportionate, and sacrificial. But this is not enough." What more should we ask people to do in order to live a life of stewardship?

Chapter 9

Taking and Giving

Stewardship calls us to be people who are willing to take and to give, and you and I have taken much. We have taken the gifts of a good and gracious God, and we are asked now to share them. The pastoral letter on stewardship does have a certain urgency. As we say in the introduction to the pastoral letter, it is addressed to us: Catholic citizens of a wealthy, powerful nation facing many questions about its identity and role in the waning years of a troubled century, members of a community of faith blessed with many human and natural resources, yet often uncertain about how to sustain them and use them.

+Thomas J. Murphy

In the early 1990s, when I was writing a column for *The Record*, the Archdiocese of Louisville's weekly newspaper, I wrote about the stewardship themes in Charles Dickens' classic story, *A Christmas Carol*. We all know the story. Ebenezer Scrooge, an embittered old miser, is confronted on Christmas Eve by a series of ghosts who help him to see his life (past, present, and future) with new eyes. Scrooge begins to see that choices he made in his early adulthood cut him off from those he loved (family, friends, and co-workers) and led him to live an angry, lonely life. Only a radical change in his attitude and behavior can save him from the wretched life he is living and from a dismal, meaningless death.

The Anti-Steward

Scrooge is the great anti-steward. His lifestyle is the opposite of what the pastoral letter tells us is characteristic of Christian stewardship. Scrooge is not grateful; he is bitter and resentful. He believes that he has earned everything he possesses (the hard way) and that he is entitled to be left alone. He accepts no responsibility for the poor or the homeless—even at Christmas. He is satisfied that the prisons and workhouses will provide for those who do not have his will to work or his business skills. He is oblivious to the working conditions of his employee, Bob Cratchit, and he is ignorant of the poverty and sickness that the Cratchit family has to endure.

Two volunteer fundraisers call on Scrooge at his place of business the day before Christmas. They are rudely shown the door. Generosity is not a priority in the business plan of Scrooge and Marley. Even Scrooge's nephew is rebuffed when he tries to invite his Uncle Scrooge to Christmas dinner. Warmth, fellowship, and hospitality are not important to Scrooge. He sees everything associated with Christmas with negative, cynical eyes, and until his encounter with the spirit world, he cannot be persuaded to open his heart and embrace the joys of the season. In the end, Scrooge recognizes the truth about himself: all of his gifts and talents have come to nothing. Unless there is a profound change, Scrooge will meet his Maker empty-handed—with nothing to show for all his years as a steward of the gifts and talents God has given him.

We know that this story has a happy ending. Scrooge sees the light. He changes his attitude and his behavior. He stops hoarding everything and starts giving. He takes responsibility for others (like Tiny Tim), and he starts sharing himself with others—time, talent, and treasure. As a result, he becomes a happy man, a good steward, and a lover of life. He finally learns to balance taking and giving. This is what stewardship calls us to be: people who are willing to take and give.

The Dead Sea and the Sea of Galilee illustrate the importance of taking and giving. What is the difference between these two bodies of water? The Dead Sea takes and does not give, and when you take and do not give, you are dead. The Sea of Galilee is a body of water that takes and gives. It is alive and teeming with the presence of vegetation and the signs of God's presence among us (RPL).

Accepting God's Gifts

The pastoral letter tells us that stewardship involves taking (accepting) the gifts that God continues to offer. Old Scrooge had shut the door on God's grace (until Marley's ghost appeared to him as the door knocker). Before his conversion, Scrooge was a taker who couldn't give.

The stewardship pastoral challenges us to be takers, who receive God's gifts gratefully, but also givers who share what we have with others out of justice and love. Stewardship calls us to see things with new eyes, to cast off our old, self-centered ways and to embrace a new way of living. Stewardship invites us to come alive (as Scrooge did) by accepting responsibility for others and by developing our gifts and talents so that we can give them back to the Lord with increase. You and I have taken much. We have taken the gifts of a good and gracious God, and we are asked now to share them.

Questions for Reflection and Discussion

1. Before his conversion, Ebenezer Scrooge was the anti-steward, a taker who couldn't give. How was Scrooge's life different after the spirits left him? What did he do to show that he was a changed man?

2. Name someone you know who is extremely generous. Is he or she a happy, joyful person or someone who's often sad or depressed? What's the connection between the way we give and the way we feel?

3. "A commitment to stewardship can change the way we live." How might a more intense commitment. to stewardship change your life? What would you do differently if you took stewardship more seriously?

Chapter 10

A Lifestyle of Sharing

The stewardship pastoral, if you look at it carefully, mentions finances twice in the entire sixty-four pages. That is not what people expected. Because stewardship, as we look at it and we reflect upon it, goes beyond sharing one's resources; it goes beyond the mere sharing of financial gifts that have been given to us. It asks us to do something far more difficult, and that is to share ourselves, to share our time, our abilities, our ministry, our relationships. Stewardship is really a call to be a holy people.

+Thomas J. Murphy

The Catholic Encyclopedia defines tithing as "the practice whereby a tenth of one's income or goods is given in support of and extension of the Christian cause." Taken from the Old English word meaning "a tenth," the practice of tithing is referenced in both the Old Testament (cf. Dt 14:22; Malachi 3:10) and the New Testament (cf. 2 Cor 8:2–6; Jas 2:17).

Many Christian denominations stress tithing, and research has shown that religious groups that require their members to tithe (or to give a substantial portion of their income) receive a greater per capita share than those that do not have this requirement. I think it stands to reason that if you make tithing a requirement for membership in a church, the majority of the members of that church will tithe—if only to maintain their status as members. Thus, the important question is not why Catholics (who are not required to tithe) give less than Mormons (who must tithe in order to remain in good standing). The real question is, what is it about the faith and spirituality of the Church of Jesus Christ of Latter-day Saints that inspires Mormons to tithe?

Why do Catholics give less than other religious groups? This question is not the important one. We have to focus instead on something far more radical, far more fundamental. We have to focus on the ways that a commitment to stewardship influences how we live. Increased giving is the result of a stewardship lifestyle—not the starting point.

Whenever someone asked Archbishop Murphy about tithing, he would respond with an anecdote that he attributed to another Chicago-born bishop, the late William J. McManus, who at the time of his service on the bishops' ad hoc committee on stewardship was the retired bishop of Fort Wayne-South Bend, Indiana.

One time at a committee meeting, [Bishop McManus] told us a story of a good friend of his who was making

$2,000 a week. This particular person, if that person tithed, would give $200 a week to the Church. That is magnificent. That is wonderful. But my friends, there is something missing. The key question is not giving the 200 bucks a week. The key question is what do you do with the other $1,800? The key question is what do you do with all of your gifts? And to measure them all only by percentage is missing the point of making stewardship a way of life (RPL).

Why was it so important to Archbishop Murphy to keep stewardship and finances separate? I believe that part of the answer is cultural. He grew up in an era when pastors (especially Irish pastors) were often accused—rightly or wrongly—of "only caring about money." Many priests of that generation reacted against this negative stereotype. They wanted to be seen as pastors, not fundraisers, and they tried to avoid at all costs any suggestion that their primary motivation for any pastoral initiative was financial.

Time and Talent

Archbishop Murphy talked about "time and talent" but he couldn't bring himself to use the word "treasure." He joked that it reminded him of Long John Silver in Robert Louis Stevenson's *Treasure Island*. The archbishop's aversion to "treasure" led him to use some awkward phrases like "time, talent, and resources." He also insisted on avoiding the word "money" whenever possible, and, as a result, he would often speak of "finances" or "financial resources" instead.

The reluctance of many clergy to talk about money in pastoral situations is a problem that needs to be addressed. (See *The Reluctant Steward Revisited*, available at www/saintmeinrad.edu/reluctantsteward.) Money is a dominant value in our contemporary culture, and it is essential that Christians learn how to deal with money in their everyday lives. A commitment to stewardship as a way of life is what makes it possible for Christians to reassess their attitudes toward their financial affairs—along with every other dimension of their daily lives. Stewardship then becomes a lifestyle of sharing. If we can recognize the importance of sharing—our hearts, our hands, and our possessions—all of the church's financial problems will be solved. The key question is what do we do with all of our gifts? And to measure them all only by percentage is missing the point of making stewardship a way of life.

Questions for Reflection and Discussion

1. Research suggests that Catholics give less to the Church than the members of many other Christian denominations. Should this be a matter of concern to Catholics? Why or why not?

2. Do you know what percentage of your income you give to the Church and to other non-profit organizations? Are you satisfied with your giving, or do you wish you could be more generous?

3. "The important question is not 'How much do I give?' but rather 'What do I do with all God's gifts?'" Do you agree or disagree and why?

Two Brothers

Let me share with you a story that gives, hopefully, a response to how we might use our resources.

Time-before-time, when the world was young, two brothers shared a field and a mill. Each night they divided evenly the grain they had ground together during the day. One brother lived alone; the other had a wife and a large family. One day the single brother thought to himself, "It isn't really fair that we divide the grain evenly. I've only myself to care for, but my brother has children to feed." So each night he secretly took some of his grain into his brother's granary to see that he was never without.

But the married brother said to himself one day, "It isn't fair that we divide the grain evenly, because I have children to provide for me in my old age, but my brother has no one. What will he do when he is old?" So every night he secretly took some of his grain to his brother's granary. As a result, both of them always found their supply of grain mysteriously replenished each morning.

Then one night they met each other half way between their two houses. They suddenly realized what had been happening all this time, and they embraced each other in love.

The story goes that God witnessed their meeting and proclaimed, "This is a holy place, a place of love, and here it is that my temple shall be built."

+Thomas J. Murphy

Chapter 11

Final Reflections

In 1996, I was invited by the editors of *New Directions for Philanthropic Fundraising*, a quarterly journal sponsored by the Center on Philanthropy at Indiana University and published by Jossey-Bass Publishers, to put together a team of writers for a monograph titled, "The Practice of Stewardship in Religious Fundraising." I accepted the invitation, and I recruited a team that included representatives from several Protestant denominations and two Catholics, Archbishop Thomas J. Murphy and Cecelia Hart Price. (Ms. Price co-edited the volume with me and wrote the final chapter, "Implications for Fundraising Professionals.")

The title of Archbishop Murphy's chapter, which was published posthumously in the fall of 1997 along with five other articles on various stewardship and fundraising themes, is "Giving from the Heart." This article was Archbishop Murphy's final opportunity to deliver his stewardship message and to give personal witness to stewardship as a way of life.

"Giving from the Heart" is based on stewardship talks he gave during the final months of his life. Many of the themes from his earlier talks are included, but they are presented very differently. The funny stories were omitted (in part because he was writing an article for a professional journal, but also because he had some very serious things to say). "Giving from the Heart" speaks to the professional philanthropic community, but it also contains profound personal reflections on stewardship—as a way of life and as a preparation for death.

> Every week or ten days I go through an experience that sustains the gift of life within me. When I go to the hospital for a transfusion, I watch the nurse begin the process, and I offer a prayer of thanksgiving to the donor who has shared his or her life with me. I stop to wonder who the person was, why that person made this gift to someone he or she would never know or meet. And I am grateful. I become aware of how the stewardship gift of another person sustains my life. And I ask again and again how I might share the gifts I have with others (GH, p. 30).

"Giving from the Heart" introduces *Stewardship: A Disciple's Response* to the professional philanthropic community. For this reason, the archbishop is careful to describe his vision of stewardship in ways that speak to a broader audience.

> I believe that *Stewardship: A Disciple's Response* presents a vision of stewardship that is relevant to the needs and concerns of all philanthropic organizations in our country today. I think this approach to stewardship would fit naturally into any leadership education curriculum, and I urge educational and community leaders to find ways to make stewardship an integral part of community service and leadership education programs (GH, p. 25).

A vision of stewardship that is relevant to all philanthropic organizations is nothing less than the conviction that our most precious possessions—life, liberty, and the pursuit of happiness (understood as a full and meaningful life)—have all been given to us as gifts to be nourished, cared for in responsible ways, and freely shared with others (GH, p. 25). Whether we recognize these gifts as coming from a good and gracious God or see them as the legacy of our American tradition, we have a responsibility to nurture these precious possessions and share them with others.

Mature Stewardship

The concept of mature discipleship (conviction #1) is explained as the way responsible citizens understand their relationship to the community, the environment, and to the abundant gifts they have received from life itself. Stewardship is expressed over an entire lifetime (conviction #2); the good steward believes that he or she is personally responsible (and accountable) for the quality of life—on this planet, in the nation, and in his or her own neighborhood. This commitment to care for others is carried out over the course of a whole lifetime.

Stewardship has the power to change the way we live (conviction #3) by transforming the determinism of political and economic systems and by calling attention to the gift of freedom and the opportunities it provides us to share with others and to build communities that are prosperous, just, and free.

Looking Back

"Giving from the Heart" provided Archbishop Murphy with an opportunity to look back over the five years since the publication of the pastoral letter. In the article, he expresses his pleasure at the growing acceptance of the pastoral letter on stewardship as an invaluable resource to aid the Catholic Church in the United States in fulfilling its mission and ministries.

Though Catholic parishes, institutions, and dioceses often initiate a commitment to stewardship in light of financial needs, it is amazing what happens when they recognize the far more basic and demanding challenge of steward-ship. When we begin to take stewardship seriously as a response of disciples of Jesus, we soon discover that the agenda switches from increased financial generosity to the radical call to faith and commitment. This radical call to faith and commitment introduces us to a spirituality that makes an impact on our lives and on the lives of the people we serve (GH, p. 26).

When we take stewardship seriously, the agenda switches from the church's resource needs to the individual Christian's need for a spirituality of daily living; from the demands of diocesan and parish ministry to the far more radical demands of trying to be a faithful follower of Jesus Christ today. This places stewardship at the very heart of Christian life and calls our attention to the far more basic and demanding challenge of stewardship, the call to be a holy people.

Archbishop Murphy's experience with leukemia in the seven months before he died confirmed his belief that a commitment to stewardship changes the way we live.

Over the past few years, I have shared [the pastoral letter's first] conviction with countless groups of people. However, my recent illness has made me aware of what it means to me.

My leukemia has been a unique cross to carry, and I am unsure how long my own way of the cross will be. Yet there are others who carry crosses far heavier than mine. I am finally beginning to appreciate the cost involved in being a disciple of Jesus.

But the nagging question is whether I am willing to pay the price. Each time I celebrate the Eucharist, which recalls the passion, death and resurrection of Jesus, I pray that I will encounter once again the God who embraced death to gain life. I pray that I will have the courage to do the same (GH, pp. 28-29).

The "conscious, firm decision" that the pastoral letter says a mature disciple makes "to follow Jesus no matter what the cost" took on a radically new meaning for Archbishop Murphy in the final years of his life. It forced him to take stewardship seriously.

The pastoral letter's second and third convictions—that it takes an entire lifetime to become a Christian steward and that stewardship has the power to effect a radical change in our lives—also spoke to Archbishop Murphy in new ways following his experience with leukemia.

> Throughout my life, I thought I had the gift of faith. Yet it often happened during the endless December nights of last year that I reflected on what my faith was asking of me. Why me? What did I do wrong? How much will I have to suffer? How long will I live?
>
> These and countless other questions haunted me throughout those long nights. Yet each day would bring a new dawn and I would remind myself that all my experiences were part of the faith that gives meaning and purpose to who I am and what I believe. My faith would tell me that what I was experiencing was part and parcel of committing myself to the person of Jesus (GH, p. 27).

The end of life brings its own choices, no longer simply focusing our attention on how we are to live, but also now inviting us to make some fundamental decisions about death. We are invited to choose not how or when or where we will die, but in what spiritual condition. Will we accept the Lord's call with faith? Will we be sustained by our hope in the resurrection? Or will we close our eyes to the reality of death—filled with anxiety and fear? It is faith that allows us to say "yes" to the gift of life, and it is faith that gives us the strength and the courage to follow Jesus through the experience of death to life everlasting. Only with faith can we pray these words of Ignatius Loyola:

Take, Lord, and receive all my liberty;
My memory, my understanding
And my entire will,
All I have and call my own.
You have given all to me.
To you, Lord, I return it.
Everything is yours; do with it what you will.
Give me only your love and your grace;
That is enough for me.

It was with these words that Archbishop Murphy concluded "Giving from the Heart": "Yes, friends, I have learned well: 'Give me only your love and your grace. That is enough for me.' And it is. For me, stewardship is not an option. It is a way of life" (GH, p. 32).

In the end, it doesn't matter who we are. It doesn't matter one darn bit what we own. What matters is our decision to follow Jesus—in spite of the cost—and to place all our trust in a good and gracious God.

Questions for Reflection and Discussion

1. How would you describe stewardship in your own words?

2. How have life's difficult experiences affected your understanding and practice of stewardship?

3. "In the end, it doesn't matter who you are or what you own." Do you agree or disagree and why?

APPENDIX

The following is a transcript of an address given by Archbishop Thomas J. Murphy in Indianapolis, Indiana on November 29, 1993.

Reflections on the Pastoral Letter,
Stewardship: A Disciple's Response

I have to admit that serving as chair of the stewardship committee for the National Conference of Catholic Bishops has been a grace and a blessing. These past few years of serving on this committee have helped me to reflect on some of the fundamental issues of what it means to be a human being, a Christian, a priest, and a bishop. It has been, and it continues to be, a quest to know more about what I must be and do to live as a disciple of Jesus, to appreciate the gifts of life, humanity, and faith.

Allow me to place the pastoral letter on stewardship in perspective. Its origin comes from a concern to meet the many needs of the church in our parishes, dioceses, country, and world. It was obvious a few years ago, and even more obvious today, that the church cannot continue its incredible outreach to meet human needs or continue the mission and ministry of Jesus in our world today without the resources so essential for the church to make a difference in health care, charities, missionary work, education, ministries, and the life of the church in our parishes, dioceses, and the world.

The resources that the church needs to continue its mission and ministry do not fall from heaven as the manna did to feed the Jewish people in their journey to the Promised Land. Rather, as we all know, the generosity of our people provides the resources for the church to fulfill the ministry of Jesus in today's world.

Yet, as the committee on stewardship reflected on the challenge of providing resources for the needs of the church, it realized quickly that people are extremely responsive to the dramatic and urgent needs that are portrayed graphically on television or through the media—whether it be the starvation in Somalia, the flooding here in the Middle West, the hurricanes that wreaked havoc in Florida, or other human disasters that come to our attention. As we all know, starvation, homelessness, poverty, and countless other human needs remain long after the television anchor people move on to a new crisis.

The Committee on Stewardship knew it could raise the consciousness of people to become aware of these dramatic needs and to encourage them to respond. The committee knew also that there are many ways in which professional fund raisers can help the church ask people for greater support. Yet, the Ad Hoc Committee on Stewardship envisioned its task as something far more radical, far more fundamental. We realized that stewardship is part of faith; it is one of the chief characteristics of what it means to be a disciple of Jesus. Stewardship is a lifestyle that reflects who we are and what we believe. It goes beyond the mere sharing of one's resources, but asks us to share ourselves—our time, our abilities, our ministry, our relationships. Stewardship is really a call to be a holy people.

The first reading in today's liturgy speaks of this challenge when Paul writes to the Thessalonians and to us by saying: "We urge you and appeal to you in the Lord Jesus to make more and more progress in the kind of life you are meant to live, the life that God wants...What God wants is for all of you to be holy" (1 Thes. 4:1–3).

Referring to the letters from St. Paul reminds me of the cartoon character called Charlie Brown, who meets Lucy as she's coming home from Sunday school. "What are you studying?" he asks. "The letters of St. Paul," she answers. "Do you like it?" he asks. "I'm not sure. I feel a little queasy about reading someone else's mail."

However, as we know, Paul's letters are not only addressed to the Thessalonians, but to all of us as well here in the twentieth century.

Principles of Stewardship

This call to be a holy people is at the heart of stewardship. Essential to stewardship are three principles that we need to appropriate within our lives. These principles are:

- Each and every baptized person is called to be a disciple of Jesus Christ. However, above and beyond this basic call to ministry and the Christian vocation, mature disciples make a conscious, firm decision, carried out in action, to be followers of Jesus Christ, no matter the cost to themselves.

- Beginning in conversion, a change of heart, this commitment is expressed not in a single action, nor even in a series of actions over a period of time, but in an entire way of life. It means committing one's very self to the Lord.

- Stewardship is an expression of discipleship with the power to change how we understand and live out our lives. Disciples who practice stewardship recognize God as the origin of life, the giver of freedom, the source of all they have and are and will be.

These principles are not new to any one of us. How do we appropriate them into our lives? How do they touch the core of who we are so that they make a difference in our lives?

I cannot ask these questions of others without asking them of myself. For me, this last year has been a significant one in my life. I turned 60 years old, and if I live until the age of 75, which would be a gift and a blessing, I suddenly realized that for every 4 years that I have lived, I have only one left—if I am fortunate. If I were 50 years of age, I could say that for every two years of life I had lived, I have one left. Why do I raise these mathematical realities in terms of life? For one reason or another, it makes me aware of the fragile and wonderful gift that God has shared with me, and I must ask how I will use the years that remain. The question so essential to stewardship takes on a new urgency: "What do I own and what owns me?"

This is a question that must be part of our lives, and we cannot just keep asking, "What does it mean?" It reminds me of the story of an anthropologist who was studying the aboriginal people in Australia. In the community in which she lived, there was a rich tradition of storytelling. The people would gather in the evening, a story would be told, and then another and another. The anthropologist felt extraordinarily privileged when she was invited to join the group.

The first story told that evening was about the ancient mythic animal ancestor of the group and its adventures in the primeval world. It was rich with detail, action, and imagery. At the end of the story, the anthropologist was delighted. "Can I ask you a question?" she said. "What does it mean?" There was silence. All eyes were on her. The elder looked at her gravely and said, "That is the one question you cannot ask." It was a long time before she was invited again. She had asked the wrong question.

Stewardship becomes a way of life when we do not have

to ask the meaning of the question, "What do I own and what owns me?" but when it becomes part of our way of life.

Qualities of Stewardship

The pastoral letter on stewardship is an opportunity especially to reflect on what it means for each one of us to be a steward in the best sense of the word. To be a steward is to be the faithful manager of what belongs to another. It is so easy to make an immediate distinction. When it comes to spiritual realities, it is very clear what belongs to God. God has given us grace, divine life, the church, redemption, the sacraments. But I am also steward of my gifts, talents, and resources, which may be recognized as my personal possessions, but when you get right down to it, anything and everything I possess, I hold in trust. I am accountable to God, and with such accountability, there come obligations.

Such accountability is a call to fidelity where I am a reliable and trustworthy steward who knows that I must use whatever gifts I possess to acknowledge a God who is faithful to me. But fidelity also calls us to be people filled with faith, people willing to say "yes" to God by saying "yes" to creation, to life, to the Gospel.

The stewardship pastoral asks us to reflect on the faith response we give to being disciples of Jesus. Faith is far more than an intellectual commitment to a set of truths, doctrine, or dogma. Faith is a response to a person. For us, it is the response to Jesus Christ, who uses the images of the steward often in parables to stress the accountability and responsibility we should have in the use of our gifts. As the pastoral letter tells us, being a steward is a whole new way of seeing who we are and what we believe.

As disciples of Jesus, men and women willing to walk with the Lord, we try to imitate the life of Christ, which is indeed challenging and even difficult in many ways. But it is also a way of life that can bring us intense joy. Such joy comes when we are willing to be collaborators with God in creation, redemption, and sanctification by our care and responsibility for the world in which we live, for human life, for the gift of time we can share with others, for the grace of ongoing conversion.

We are also stewards of the church in its ongoing mission to continue the ministry of Jesus among us. As stewards of the church, we foster and cherish the gifts of all people while using our own gifts to serve the community of faith. Stewardship within the church calls us to evangelization by proclaiming the good news, as well as asking us for our support of the church's institutions and programs. In turn, we must call the church at all levels to live out the stewardship it teaches by accountability and responsibility for its finances and resources.

Good stewardship also requires parishes and dioceses to use the gifts of personal service and witness of people in their involvement with the church through consultative structures. The Eucharist becomes the sign and symbol of stewardship for the individual Christian and the church. In the Eucharist, we celebrate the renewal of the covenant Jesus made with us, but we, in turn, renew our covenant with him as well as with one another. The Eucharist is the sign and expression of solidarity of God with the human race, and the human race with God and one another. We bring our lives, our gifts, our resources to the altar, and they too must be transformed as the bread and wine are transformed into the body and blood of Jesus.

Stewardship—A New Way of Seeing
Stewardship is a far more radical challenge than the sharing of our resources with the church. There is no doubt that it is

important to ask people to live a life of stewardship that is prayerful, planned, proportionate, and sacrificial when it comes to sharing one's resources with one's parish, diocese, and the universal church. But no program, no choice of words, no stewardship appeal slogan, no brochure, no letter from the pastor or even from the bishop will have any long-term effect on the lives of people to encourage them to live a life of stewardship if the far more fundamental issue of faith and conversion is not addressed. Again, it is a whole new way of seeing, living, and being.

Stewardship does require a new vision. The late Canadian artist, William Kuralek, painted a series of nativity scenes in which the child, Mary, and Joseph are situated as extraordinary characters within the most commonplace, ordinary scenes. There is the Christ Child as an Inuit child, cuddling a Husky pup in the shelter of an igloo. There is the Christ Child as a black baby, held by a black Mary as they sit at a table at a Salvation Army Christmas dinner for homeless people. There is the Christ Child as a native Canadian seeking shelter for the night.

The scenes, which are described as dreams of the artist as a child, are gathered into a collection entitled *A Northern Nativity*. Each painting is accompanied by the artist's written reflections. At the outset of the book, Kuralek writes these haunting words of our calling to see the Christ Child among people of our own time:

If it happened here
   as it happened there...
If it happened now
   as it happened then...
Who would have seen the miracle?
Who would have brought gifts?
Who would have taken them in?

The stewardship vision is the ability to see with eyes of faith the need to share our resources, time, talents, and possessions in ways that enable us to recognize Christ's presence among us in who we are and the gifts of time, talent, and resources that we share.

The Challenge of Stewardship

The pastoral letter points out well that consumerism and materialism shape so many of our lives, often in contrast to the values of the Gospel. It is so easy to seek meaning in possessions, work, status. We measure ourselves and others in terms of what we have instead of who we are. We are caught in the struggle between life as giving and life as getting.

In the Scriptures, there are constant references to two bodies of water—the Dead Sea and the Sea of Galilee. Two thousand years ago, the Dead Sea was dead, and it still is today. Two thousand years ago, the Sea of Galilee was alive, teeming with fish. It is still alive today. The difference between these two bodies of water is that the Dead Sea takes—and does not give. The Sea of Galilee takes and gives.

The image of these two bodies of water calls us to be alive as well by a commitment to simplicity, service, and sharing.

The pastoral letter on stewardship is not a new program that will yield incredible financial results for parishes, institutions, and needs of the Christian community. Rather, the pastoral letter is an invitation to reflect on one's faith and what our faith asks us to be and to do.

The pastoral letter on stewardship does have a certain urgency about it. As we say in the introduction to the pastoral letter, it is addressed to us—Catholic citizens of a wealthy, powerful nation facing many questions about its identity and role in the waning years of a troubled century, members of a community of faith blessed with many human and material resources, yet often uncertain about how to sustain and use them.

I am sure we can identify with the rabbinical tale of the great rabbi who was dying:

The great rabbi was dying, and, as we all know, deathbed wisdom is the best. So his students lined up, single file, to receive his last words. The most brilliant student was at his bedside, the second most brilliant immediately behind him, and so on until the line ended at a pleasant fellow who was a good room and a half away.

The most brilliant student leaned over the slowly slipping rabbi and asked, "Rabbi, what is the meaning of life?" The rabbi groaned, "Life is a river." The most brilliant student turned to the second most brilliant student. "The rabbi said, 'Life is a river.'" And the word was whispered from student to student until it arrived at the pleasant enough fellow who was biting his nails a room and a half away. "What does the rabbi mean, 'Life is a river'?" he said. And the word was passed back up the line until the most brilliant student once again leaned over the slowly slipping rabbi. "Rabbi, what do you mean, 'Life is a river'?" The rabbi shrugged, "So, maybe it's not a river."

We could well feel like the students gathered around the bedside of the slowly slipping rabbi, and we could well ask the same question, "What is the meaning of life?"

The pastoral letter on stewardship tries to respond to this fundamental question by asking us to take the risk to become disciples of Jesus who dare to take the risk, who dare to dream, who dare to live out the implications of being such a disciple and living a life of stewardship. It is not a program; it is not a religious diet or exercise plan; it is not a series of set formulae we are asked to follow. It is a way of life.

Christopher Fry expresses it best when he writes:

Dark and cold we may be
    but this is no winter now,
The frozen misery of centuries breaks, cracks,
    begins to move.
The thunder is the thunder of the floes,
    the thaw, the floods, the upstart Spring.
Thank God our time is now
    when wrong comes up to face us everywhere,
    never to leave us till we
    take the longest stride of soul men ever took.
Affairs are now soul-sized.
The enterprise is exploration into God.

Thank God our time is now. Stewardship is an enterprise that invites us into an exploration of a new world—an exploration into God.